A Story Book:
A Story Spanning 8 Years

Jay
Iluminada

Copyright © 2021 Jay Iluminada

All rights reserved.

ISBN: 978-0-578-98683-8

Acknowledgements: I want give the biggests thank you to my best friend, Kathleen for allowing me to take this step with my writing and for being so supportive throughout my entire process ; Most of all for being grateful for receiving the very first (handwritten) copy of this book as a surprise birthday gift on August 6, 2020. Love you always, Jay ♥.

For anyone who has inspired me.

Passion

Writing isn't my passion.
Writing isn't my hobby
Writing is my escape.

My escape from crying.
My escape from you.
My escape from the world.

An Escape. From myself,
From all the things that
make me wanna Cry,
Or run,
Or hide,

An expression.
Of my emotions
My thoughts
My heart and soul.

If someone asked me
to show them, what
my heart contains
I'd only be able to show them words.

*Writing isn't my passion.
Or a hobby.
It's a necessity,
it's all I know.*

Chapter One: Key stone

Different eyes

Through my eyes,
I see that time flies
Watching the skies,
day by day,
daydreaming and
dreams at night

Looking at life through
different eyes
at what could've been,
what it could be
watching the dark night skies
as clouds roll by
time ticks faster
as the day goes by

watching the days pass
as you realize
not everything you do
will please
everyone
Sometimes not even
yourself.

We're not dating

I said I was done
writing about you,
I lied,
by accident.

I'm Over you,
my Romantic feelings
no longer stand,
But my love
Stands;
Strong.

I Love You.
But I don't think you see that,
All of the times
I've told you
how much you mean to me,
you've said "I know, I understand"
I Don't think you
"Know and Understand"

How dare you……
Call me early one morning
to tell me
"I Can't talk to you anymore,
my girlfriend doesn't like it"

After all those years of friendship?
after everything we've been through,
How many times have I forgiven you?
I don't want to hold anything against you,

But I will tell you,
that girl you got
She ain't no good,

No. I don't know her,
I don't even know her name but,

I know what you've said about her,
how you guys argue
a lot,
I know her voice,
her voice saying
"I don't like the way you text
my man"
the heart emojis and paragraphs,
Saying "my room smells like you"
That shit ain't cute,
I don't got no other man
in my phone like that…"

No. I don't know her.
I Do know,
She thinks she can control you

though,
I know that
She thinks you'll let her.
I know
you don't like Conflict
that you won't Fight her
when She's Wrong
Not fight with Fists, but
Words to Stand your Ground
with,

Sure,
"you gotta do
what you gotta do
to make your relationship work"
And "We're not dating"
And "you're not choosing anyone over anyone"
And "She's been there when you needed her"

Cuz obviously,
I ain't Shit,
I "wasn't" there over the summer
when you needed me
when you called, telling me, you needed me
I "wasn't" there with you at 4am
on the phone
half asleep
when you called

with an instrumental blasting in the background
telling me you were writing
and needed my opinion
on your word choice,
flow
et cetera
I can go back
to when I "wasn't there for you"
the time you "weren't" fighting with your mom,
when you "didn't" call me everyday for support
or just wanting me to lift your spirits

Let's make it seem like
I was Never there.
I Never told you
how much you mean to me,
Let's pretend.
Pretend you don't mean anything to me,
because in that case,
I've lost so many friends,
in the past year
that,
what's One more?

I said I was done
writing about you,
I accidentally lied,
because for some reason

that girl
you're "with" doesn't like me.
She Can't fathom the idea
Of You
Having a Friend
of the Opposite sex,
her insecurities irritate me.

I Only want
what's best
for You

But "We're Not Dating"
so who am I
to try to be there for You?

Obviously
I'm Wrong.

I'll let you ask your "girl",
How much you mean
to me,
But I bet
She Won't know
Or
Care,

But according to you

"You Know and Understand"
So I guess,
I'll take your word for it.

You were my Teddy Bear

Remember
in the beginning
when I was head over heels for
you ?
When I held you up on a pedestal?
Remember those times when you
had to break the news to me,
the news that-
Remember all those times
that
I forgave you?
because I do.

Remember when
you told me
I Love You
and I felt it was true?
Remember after everything we went through
how I finally figured out
I Loved You too?
Even though at the time,
I thought it was too late
I cried for days
because I was the one
who called it quits
because you said

"I don't want to do this"
over and over until, it drove me
crazy,
 until
I believed it
and I told you " it's over"
we tried to be friends -
Remember when we got back together
I was the happiest girl on Earth
because my baby was once again mine,
and I promised not to fuck it up,
I definitely do remember that.
I hope you do too;

Everything just seemed so
perfect
like out of a fairytale book
A beautiful princess and her handsome prince
finally together after all the struggles they went
through
for one another

But
Remember what happened after our one year
anniversary
when you gave me that promise ring
and promised you'd never hurt me?
You did,

hurt me
made me believe
that ring you gave me,
meant nothing.

No matter,
I stayed
I loved you.
like I never loved anyone before
I never knew what love was
before I loved you
So again I forgave you
and we moved on

Now,
here comes my part,
Remember
(I'm positive you remember as this is something
you hate and will never forgive me for)
when everything was great,
but this time I had to break some
news to you,
Now I don't think there's a need
for me to repeat it
you and I both know what it is.
but remember when I told you
you were heart broken
I could see it in your eyes;

Now as you're reading this poem
I know you wanna cry.
but this is me
once again, asking for your forgiveness,
not just for that,
but for everything else
because you need to forgive me
in order to move on.

Look,
I've accepted
there's no more chances for us
And honestly it's probably better that way.

I have one more thing
to say though,

Remember when we were dating,
A month into our relationship,
you asked me to meet your mom?
Remember I said no?
I was afraid that you'd bring me home,
and then our relationship would soon
wither away
I didn't want her to know me and then
we
didn't work out
I didn't want

to be
that girl
that always came around
and then suddenly disappeared.
But look it happened anyway...
and where are we now?

Free

His smile
is enough
to fill me
with warmth,
fluttering butterflies
in my tummy,
And a smile of my own.

His company Is enough
to make the world feel like,
it stops.

When I'm with him,
all of my problems
drop-
To the floor.
I don't have to
pick them up
because he does it for me.
He refuses to let me carry
the weight
of the world,
on my shoulders.

When I'm with him
He makes me

Want
to give him
All of me.

I mean Every little piece.
Emotionally,
Mentally and
Physically.
He makes me
forget that reality is a thing.

The fact that he listens to me
is Amazing,
It's a rare thing,
that you don't just find anywhere.

Our conversations aren't
a one way street,
He opens up to me
in a way that I admire
So much.
Because I can tell he has a wall up
and when we talk
he tells me somethings that
I'm sure
he never intended on saying
in the beginning.

I admire his ability to just take
away my stress,
And my thoughts,
to leave me feeling
like an open book;
I don't know how he does it,
I'm so sure that
I have an emotional wall built around me
But somehow
he knows how to get around it
or through it,
He has a way
of making me tell him
Everything
I'm thinking.

When I'm with him
my shyness automatically disappears.

I like him,
And I'm sure he knows this;

With him
I feel like I don't have
to hide
anything.

I know he doesn't understand

the extent
To which I appreciate him
But that's the point in this poem

I want you to know that
I'm always here for you
and even though
it's only been a few
Months,
I appreciate you
And
all of your efforts to make me feel like
the most amazing thing on this Earth,
Regardless of what anyone thinks,

You are truly amazing!

Chapter two: When you Love

4 letters = 1,000 emotions

Love
The four letter word
that will have you thinking why am I here?
and everything in between
And when you feel like you love him;
you wanna be the one for him to lean on
when
he can't lean on himself

And when love is too powerful of a word
for any human being to understand
We all push it away instead of embracing the power
of a four letter word
Love

Chicken

Running recklessly into moving traffic
on a highway without stop lights;
bound to get hit
the only question is when?
Because survival is only temporary
playing this game of love

My bed

My heart feels heavy as I lay here
I want your body next to mine
Making it feel like everything is alright
And as long as I never leave
neither will you
I want you beside me
to know I'm the only one on your mind
And no matter what you have to figure out by yourself
I'll always be the girl you turn to
because you know I'll be there to comfort you
when you need it
hold your hand if you need me to
keep that smile on your face
let you confide in me
or keep your thoughts from scrambling

My heart feels heavy as I lay here
I want your head on my chest
So I can play with your hair,
as I listen to you talk
or you listen to me talk
because we both know I'm a chatterbox
Full of many endless stories
But we always seem to make each other laugh
And I like that

We never let the mood get too heavy
without a smile or a giggle
And I like that too,
Probably part of the reason I was attracted to you
to begin with

Besides your big bug eyes and the
way you smile
Your annoying laugh
especially when it sounds fake
you've heard it all before but
for some reason right now
my heart feels heavy and
I want you next to me

Change

It was always me and you...
ONLY...
I understand the things going on
in your life are New...
As well as Mine.
Sometimes...We just need that
Me and You time
But NOW I don't know
It's like you forgot about Me
Yeah... You have your own things going on
But so do I
I don't understand what happened
You've changed
Yeah I still love you for you
But I just don't know
I feel so abandoned
Change is good in some ways
and some bad
But as of NOW I just don't know
What it is.
Sometimes I just need you just to
talk.
Please don't make things
 CHANGE.

Fell

Lead me on
Turn me on
make me fall for you
break my guard down
to tell me you don't
feel the same way

You had me
in your arms
you told me all the right things
had me thinking I was special
I thought it was true
come to find out
it was a lie

Then I ask you
tell me you don't know

Ask to explain
answer is I can't

I try to find out
what's on your mind
but you avoid me
Can't even make eye contact

Where we go from here
tell you
it's on you
you turn and
tell me it's on me
as if you don't know
the answer

I fell for you
I fell hard
but you
you
weren't there to catch me

Pouring rain

Standing here
in the rain
all I feel is pain

You held me up
in the shining sun
now that you disappeared
all I know is fear

left me in the depths
of these dark clouds
Can't get a light to shine through

you were the one
who held me up
and kept me together
now I'm down and blue
under the weather

Could never imagine
the one being hurt was me
but now I'm standing here
in the pouring rain
with all this pain
felt in my heart
all of these thoughts left in my brain

thoughts of what we could've been
thoughts of becoming more

But now that you're gone
all I feel is pain
and
I'm left
in the pouring rain
alone 💧

Swim

You see
I once too
was told
"baby girl I'll hold your hand
and I'll never let go.
We'll get through this together"
and everything in between.
" we can jump into the ocean
and we will swim together",
but then I looked around
and he
he
Was afloat at the top
watching the clouds roll by
while me,
well I,
was at the bottom
I,
was drowning
He
let me go
and I didn't know
how to swim on my own.
I watched all the words he said
float up to the top,
they float right beside him.

**And that day
was when I learned how to swim,
on my own**

Face it

It was hard
Because I did
want Everything
with you

Everything we talked about:
A house
A home
Kids
and a Family
Both Mine and Yours Combined

So when it came,
that time,
the time when
you felt that
you had to say Goodbye
All I could do was cry

And I did;
for Days on end
until I Couldn't
stand
to look at Myself in the Mirror;
view Nothing,
but an Empty feeling

Nothing. but puffy eyes
and a color Whiter than White
But Red as a tomato
at the same time

I Had to lick my battle scars
until they healed.
I was Alone.

Lonely.
For a very long time
Because I
was unwanted
for the first time
in years

Lies

The truth?
I'm scared to see you
I don't know
what my initial reaction will be

I don't know if
I'm gonna wanna
Hug you
OR kiss you,
Or hit you,
yes I know that's a bit violent,
it's a terrible habit,
You know this,
or at least
I think you do

I don't know if
I won't be able to stop thinking about the time we had sex
OR
when I was at your house
Cuddling and leaning into your chest
OR
if I'll be distracted
by all the thoughts of
how much I want that again

I don't know
if I'm gonna wanna
pour my heart out to you,
but why would I do that?
My hopes and feelings
will probably be forced to go down
the drain anyway,
maybe, that's just my pessimistic thinking
but,

We haven't had
An Actual conversation
in months
Last thing
I figured out
was that
you had a Girlfriend
and, this isn't to hold that against you,
but this is the Truth.

The Truth?
I told myself
when these feelings came to surface
I'd always want
what's best for you
that's what's important
First

Over Anything,
but that's been so hard for me
Because the part of me
that Wants to be
Your Girlfriend, Can't help but think
What if…?

The Truth?
All of me misses you,
The you that I Know

I'm Scared to see you

I wrote about this already.

but the fact is
that feeling will never change.

Because
for months on end,
I waited for the day,
I would hear you ask me
those couple of words
"Would you like to be my girlfriend?
officially?"

The day you kissed me
I was oblivious
to the fact that
my feelings
would evolve.
But as time went by,
I watched them grow
And didn't want them to stop.

The hugs,
The phone calls,
The weekend visits,
The kisses.

I allowed myself to get used to it,
All of it.
Allowed myself to get used to You
always being there,
To become attached to You,

it all seemed fine,
Until You
decided that
I
wasn't what you wanted.
I make this sound like
the biggest heartbreak of my life
that's only because I was hopeful-

But that's only because
you planted those ideas in my head,
I didn't have a problem with that
It all seemed amazing.

Then we stopped talking and
everything seemed to go downhill,
I really don't know why.

I'll always love you though.

I'll see you soon.

But I'm scared to
see you,

Because those butterflies
that I used to get
in my tummy every time
I was around you,
I think they're gone,
and I don't know if they'll return
when I see your face,

For the first time in months,
I don't want them anymore...

Rewritten

"The truth
I'm scared to see you
I don't know what my initial reaction
will be
I don't know if I'm gonna wanna
Hug you or kiss you";
Or tell you I was right
See the last time I wrote about this
My heart was hurting confused on when
you'd come back
waiting for the day to arrive

Now
The truth
I'm scared
to hear from you
the day my phone dings,
a message
lights up on my screen
with your name at the top
I don't know what I have to say to you
Or if you deserve words at all
I think you took them all
In through one ear out through the other
years and Years of the same cycle
And I'm sorry to say

You don't deserve me anymore
You don't deserve for me
to be engulfed in you
engulfed
In your every move
wondering what you're up to
I'm sorry for you
Because I tried
To be your friend
when I felt you needed me
I'm sorry to say that
My friendship
Has withered away
I hope you blame no one but yourself
And see that in the end I was right
We had Two roads
seems we took the wrong One
I'm sorry to say you've used all your Chances
And welcome backs

So when you want to Call on me
I'll no longer be around
You're welcome.
Back.

Chapter Three: Staggered thoughts

You were.....

Once upon a time
I wanted to know you
Once upon a time
your secrets intrigued me
But that was before
before I knew you were deceiving me
Before I knew
that you only ever told me half of the truth

Draft 1

"I once told you
you were my everything that you
meant the world to me"
And now that someone else is in
that place
you see what I wanted
to give you
tell me you love me
And expect a reply like
"I miss you"
or
"I still want this"
Want to show me the guy
you can be
the guy who
takes care of me
But that's off the table

Yes I woke up
thinking of you the other day
less you-
more of how I will always be proud-

Yet
I don't miss you
I wish you the best

and I'm so happy
I don't cry
late at night because of you
anymore
Don't need to wonder if you're playing me
holding on to me while being
in another's arms

Remains

Someone I used to rely so
heavily on
your chest used to be my
grace, my hands on it
as I leaned up to kiss
you and yet I was played
in front of my face
and I watch you slip
away
the slither of a friendship
that I thought was the
remains of a romance
that never existed

Blinded

If I told you I love you I was wrong
because you
weren't there yet
And when I held your hand and felt like
everything
was okay I was wrong because you didn't feel
that
And when I laid next to you to feel safe
I was wrong because you didn't see that

Move forward

It's hard to keep keeping on when
your name constantly pops up
everywhere
And your face comes up in my dreams
the words "I miss you" leaving my lips
or yours

Tower of strength

I want to be held in your embrace,
hold your hand while walking down the street
and give you kisses whenever I see your face.

I want to encourage you
to do your very best
and be there whenever you call my name.

I want to hold up 80
when you can only handle 20.
I want you to hold 80 when I can't.

I want to make you smile
and laugh.
Annoy you in a way you'll love.

Tear away

But when I strip all of that away
Can you honestly say
you love me

Lucid

I lay here sleeping dreaming of you with me
On top of me kissing me
I can feel your body and your touch
All the passion in your love
Open my eyes to find I'm only dreaming
In my dream I still didn't tell you I love you
no matter how much I wanted to
Wake up to see my to do list of kissing you
still isn't complete
because it was actually a dream within a dream
And our plans of kissing and talking about my
graduate plans were not complete
Because you were not on top of me kissing me
I was only dreaming

Food for my heart

The words on my page
Make you second guess me
Second guess yourself
The food for thought never seemed to
feed me enough
seemed to get burned
thrown in the trash and tossed away
The colors of your tie dye pancakes
mixed too weirdly
You threw them in the trash bin
The food you would feed me
Never seemed like enough
Never seemed that I was happy with
who you were
becoming

Your food for thought
Seemed like the wrong food for my heart
and I tried to make you feel appreciated
Tell you that your messed up pancake mix
was always good enough
for me
And your food for thought was food for my heart
And whatever you did was perfect
Nothing needed Manipulation
To please me

Because you had already pleased me with your ways of trying
Your food lay in the trash bin
The aroma filling the kitchen with food
For my thought
That I never consumed
Because you thought you weren't good enough

Chapter Four: Moments

Moment

Freeze this moment
just me and you
Keep us together
together like crazy glue

When I'm in your arms
I feel your love
as it carries my stress away
picks my heart up
and brightens my day

Keep us together
just me and you

Keep me here
frozen in this moment
where it feels like
it's only you and I

Keep us together
me and you
and never
leave my side

But if there ever comes a time
where you and I can't be together

Keep me in your heart
there I'll stay forever

For now
freeze this moment
with
just you and I

Night Breeze

The Sky dark
and a nice fall breeze
Comes through my window
I lay on my room floor
texting you
reading "I made up my mind,
US
Only friends"
as I read this, I am torn to pieces.

You have beaten me
with a metal baseball bat
waited for me to fall…
So you can kick me while I'm down,
yet I still managed to get up
with the little strength that I have
to rebuild myself.

Then you waited for me to cover up
my wounds,
you didn't let them fully heal
to beat me down
Once again
and again
and again
and again,

but you will watch me get up,
as my strength fades.

But this time you've beaten me so hard
that I'm not sure if I can get up
as my strength seems to fade
I'm not sure I'm strong enough anymore
you've taken
All of my strength.

So right now,
I lay on my room floor
with a night breeze coming through my window
trying to regain my Strength.

Words

I look back on the messages
when you told me
"Everything will be okay,
Our bond will never fade"
that feels like
it was Decades
ago

Before you left

Now

I miss you so much
and I want you to miss me back
but since we're just friends
you probably don't miss me like that

Answer

"Question,
Do you only write about me?"
No!
"Good cuz that's stressful…
not for me,
for you"

You think I LIKE
having you on my mind
all the time?
You think I LIKE
Thinking about you every night before bed?
I'd rather be thinking about
rainbows and unicorns or
stressing about what
I'm gonna be doing tomorrow

You think I LIKE having these feelings
for you?
You think I LIKE not knowing
how to feel
all the time?
You think I LIKE having days when
I can't stop smiling because I feel
love struck?
Days when I CAN'T get you off my mind,

Do you think I enjoy that?

This was never supposed to happen
I'd rather rewind back
to
when
we were only friends
but barely talking

Okay I lied,
too far maybe
after
we made up
and slowly started talking again
when these feelings were suppressed,
they probably weren't even a thing yet,
doesn't matter because
we can't rewind time

And now I'm stuck
thinking about you all the time
which reflects in my writing
but only you know it's about you
Cuz you know I have feelings for you

Oh wow
I just told everyone
Oh well,

that's beside the point

Do you think I LIKE
not knowing what my feelings
are going to lead to?
Not knowing if you feel this way too?
And questioning if I'd actually want to be
with you?
You think I LIKE wondering if a relationship
will change everything? And
Questioning if
You and me can ever be a thing?

Because the answer is NO,
I don't only write about you
only when you're on my mind
which nowadays
is practically all the time

Does that answer your question?

One conversation; a thousand words

"I don't know! Okay!"
I don't know
I don't know
I don't know how to express my feelings
I don't know how to say what's on my mind

"I can't seem to say what I want or
mean, I don't want it to come out wrong"
I know what I want
Do I?
Do I want to be alone?
Yes I do
I want to be alone
Do I?
I just want to be happy!

"I know that I love you"
WHAT is the definition of love?
WHY are you even questioning that?
you KNOW HE'S the ONLY one
you've EVER LOVED
the only one who made you feel
like YOU ARE
worth something
Something more than you could ever imagine

"You make me so happy"
does he really?
he does
when he's not being an ass or ignoring me,
I just can't believe
I put up with so much…
that's right,
I put up with so much
It's just Crazy
what I put MYSELF through
for HIM
would I ever be okay,
if we were to break up?
how would I feel?
what would I do?
I DON'T KNOW

"I want to be with you, and I'm sorry
for hurting you"
I am really sorry
things just tend to happen
it wasn't an accident
I just didn't intend for things to happen
that way
I don't even want to think about this

"I wish I knew how to make this
better, but I don't - I don't know. "

Don't tell

He told me
"Don't worry baby girl you'll be okay"
As tears rolled down my face

I don't want this
I don't want to be with you
I don't want to be yours

I cried
Each tear rolling down slowly
As he embraced me in his arms
held my face to his
Puckered his lips
brought them closer to mine
until they touched

His touch
gave me
Goosebumps
like the ones you get
in the wind of a winter night
when you just want to hide
Under your covers and hope
you never
have to go outside again

"It's okay"
His deep voice whispered in my ear
"Calm down"
When all I wanted to hear was
it's over now

Quiet

All I hear is silence
Silence
we're talking
in the middle of conversation
but all I hear is silence

I'm silent
"You there?"
Silence
"Hello?"

"Oh yeah…"

Chapter Five: For You

Nightlight

Your heart guarded.
Hid in that little crack
between the bed and the wall
that little crack
that you lose things in
and can never find again

Your feelings hid
in that crack
along with your heart
To a place where
we can't find them

My feelings
hidden
In plain sight
In the dark they'll glow
like a night light;

The room is dark
I can't see your feelings
only the glow
of my own
Reflecting on to you
making me feel better
like I'm not the only one feeling

this way

The glow that I know
is only my own
but I pretend we share
so I can feel like you
care about me
in the way I want you to

But in the morning
when the sun comes up
my glow is
Gone

Your feelings still
Gone

In the End
I don't know
what you think of me

I haven't told you this yet;

You lit a fire in me,
gave me
the leeway to feel more confident.
Taught me
how to smile more,
how to
admire how beautiful I am.

The way you admire
me is amazing;
You may not even know that you're doing it
but you are;
Telling me to smile;
making me smile.
Taking pictures of me smiling,
and keeping them.

Your views of me,
are something
I've never heard from anyone else.
The way you were able to see through me
within the first 2 days
of speaking to me
is something
I've never seen
anyone be able to do;

I
Think
You're
Sweet.
Thoughtful.
Kind.
Giving.
Loving.
Cute.
Pure Gold.
a Treasure.

I think
you came into my life
for the same reason I came into yours;
To improve is
To stick through it,
no matter how long this lasts.

Our talks make me want to stay
around you.
We can talk about something new every 2
seconds,
get confused,
Then laugh.

Being around you everyday,

Showed me so many different things,
Things that I wouldn't
have been able to see otherwise.

The way you write
a new page
in your book of life
EveryDay
Never ceases to amaze me.
I can't help but wonder
what chapter I'll be in
and when it'll Officially Begin
or if it'll End before the Start.

Everytime we kiss
I want to stay there forever;
Feel the pounding of my heart.

Everytime you make me smile
I get butterflies.
I panic.
I know what that feeling is;

The feeling of wanting you
to stay
in that one moment
with that one person.

The feeling of relaxation,
of feeling safe,
of feeling like
I can stay all day , in that one place.

The feeling
of Feelings
that I can't seem
to explain.

Feelings

Lately,
your smile
has made me smile
more than ever

I can stare at one picture
all day.
Yes, that's a bit weird
but seeing You happy
Makes Everything in My world okay.

When you're sad
or mad,
I want to
take all of your pain away
bring back your smile
that I love

That I love;
I almost told you
I Love You
the other day but didn't.
In some ways I'm sure I do.
but I don't
want that change
anything

between me and you.
I like how
open we are with Each Other.
how I Don't have to hide Anything.
I don't want any of that to disappear
Because of those 3 Words.

I Love You.
In many ways
as a friend,
as someone I truly treasure.
as someone to talk to.
To hold.
To be there for.
To love.

Yes I can see a future with you.
I want to help you grow
be there through it all.
Help you cope with your past
in a way that
you can accept.

I hope you can accept that
My feelings are strong
and I don't know what to do
other than let that be known.

I still don't know
if I want to tell you
I Love You.

__Your voice, only a whisper__

" If I ever hurt you, I'm sorry,
I didn't come into your life to fuck it up "

" If I ever hurt you I'm sorry "
my heart beats out of my chest .
I can't face you,
the river is rolling , blurring up my eyes
And I sit and wonder how much
I mean to you ,
why you care about me ,
or if you care about me at all .

I listen as more words
leave your lips
your voice sounding like a whisper
in my brain
I nod every now and then
to let you know I'm listening .

I can't remember what else
you said
only those words
"If I ever hurt you I'm sorry"

The weight of tons
sits on my chest

I choke up

" If I ever hurt you I'm sorry "
on repeat in my brain they allow me to feel more
than I was willing to
in the beginning
those words are stuck
in my head
And I can't get them out ;

Sweet .
Caring .
Thoughtful .
All adjectives I use to describe you ,
And I don't wanna ever think
that isn't true .
Don't sugar coat the truth
ever
I beg you

You've seen all of me
Seen what I'm like behind closed doors
I'm vulnerable around you

" If I ever hurt you , I'm sorry "
And I can say
the same to you

" If I ever hurt you , I'm sorry "
but I plan to be here
for a long time
and my intentions aren't to hurt you
but to be the one to lift your spirits
When you're down
make you smile when you feel like you can't
and be everything you imagined I could be .

I plan to be here for a long time
and once I set my mind to something
I always pull through

just don't doubt me
I got you ♡

Insure Me

Can you tell me
everything I need to know
tell me about your childhood
and how and where you grew up
tell me about your mom
dad,
brother,
sisters,
you.

You.
you.
Tell me about you
tell me about who you are,
What you like to do
and what you're used to

Tell me it all
tell me the truth,
no lies.
tell me who you are, underneath,
all your smiles and jokes.

Tell me who you are
as a person,
tell me where you were born

tell me when it happened
tell me about you
just you,
just

You
just

You and me
tell me about us
tell me,
What you want this to be,
tell me
if you want me,
or if you don't.

Tell me
Your feelings,
feelings about life,
feelings about work,
and dance,
everything you love.
Your feelings about me
tell me those,
tell me
am I the one you want to be with
or are there others?

Tell me everything,
Just tell me
I want to know it all …
Past,
Present,
Future,
Tell me about what you see in the future.

Just tell me
I just
want to know
I just want to know the truth

Just tell
tell me
Everything

I'm Hear

Can you tell me Everything I need to know?
Tell me about your childhood
and where you grew up
Tell me about your fam
what's your relationship like with them?

Tell me about
You.
Tell me about
Who You Are.
about what Scares you

Tell me the Truth
don't lie or sugarcoat
Tell me who you are Underneath
all your smiles and jokes

Tell me about you as a Person
Your views of Yourself
your favorite things about Yourself
All of the Things that make You.
You.

just You.
Just
You;

Just
You and Me.
Tell me about Us
about what you want this to be.
Tell me if you want me;

Tell me your feelings;
about life,

What kind of person do you aspire to be?

Tell me about the things you Love.
Tell me about the people you Love.
about what makes you happy

Tell me Everything…
Everything I know,
tell me over again.
Tell me Everything I don't
so I can hear it for the first time
and let it soak in.

Tell me about your Past,
about what's going on Now,
about what you see 5 years from Now
and Everything beyond that.

Tell me

Everything
And I promise
I'll listen
even if you feel like
Nobody wants to

Chapter Six: You're Beautiful

Dare

Dare to dream
Dream to dare
Dream of daring
Dream a new dream
Dream of telling the truth
Dream of
Living free
Being you
Showing your own style
Dream of things your own way
Showing the world
Showing who you really are

6 things about you

1. Your Eyes
   big
   bright
   Looking Softly into the distance

2. Your Lips
   soft
   Kissable
   forming that Beautiful smile

3. Your Smile
   beautiful
   inviting
   Heart warming

4. Your Heart
   hard to reach
   hidden
   sweet
   caring
   makes you Thoughtful

5. Your Mind
   always thoughtfully
   thinking
   a mind full of Wonderful thoughts

6. Your Personality
   Wonderful
   Big
   Bright
   Beautiful
   Heart warming
   Loving
   Just like you

What if I told you…

I can tell
you're beautiful
but you don't seem to
know that
do you?
Your life story
is one that's hard to understand
so you assume
that no one can
But maybe
Just maybe
that isn't true.

What if
I
want
to understand you?
What if I want
to know EVERYTHING
about you?
Learn about you,
just like you're Still learning about yourself,
or Maybe more
by watching you grow.

What if I want to see through

all of your pain
just see you for you ?

What if
I told you
these questions
aren't what if's ?
They're not .
they're what I want to do

'Cause you see ;
Again
I almost told you "I love You"

I almost
told you
I love you
on multiple occasions
while you were lying beside me
Holding my hand
just being you

I almost told you
I love you
on multiple occasions
For just being you

'Cause the feelings you give me

when I'm around you are
unexplainable;

It's the smile you put on my face
And all of your annoying ways
It's the way I laugh when I'm around you
And the warmth I feel when I'm beside you
the way my cheeks turn red
when I hear your voice
saying my name
your willingness
to know and understand who I am
and what made me this way

It's your smile .
and the squint that goes along with it;
your laugh .
How it sounds pretend
when you're in certain situations .
It's the confusion on your face
when I do weird and random things
It's your willingness to try
new things

It's You .
as a person .
I can tell
You know you're not perfect

You don't try to be;
You know perfect is just a facade
In a world where
that's what everyone strives to be

But in a bunch of ways you
Are perfect
to me
I think you're amazing
Although
I still haven't seen all of you
yet

These are the reasons
I've almost told you
I love you
on multiple occasions
Well at least
The ones I could list

Dark Room

I crave your thrust
Slowly drilling -
The back and forth motion as I grab your waist with
excitement
dragging my nails up your back
As I arch into you

I crave your touch
Your fingers sliding over my soft skin
Sliding your fingers
One by One
Into my ocean
Overwhelming me with pleasure

I crave your inches
Slowly inching into me
Quickening my breath
As my sense become more intense

I crave
Your lips
Your soft
Supple kisses
Slowly
touching my lips ,

Touching my neck,
my legs
and everything in between

I crave you
Your hands
Your hands in mine,
Holding tight like we'll never let each other go

Never fall into a darkness that will hurt
Only this dark room where we lie
Ready to feel the pounding
of our hearts
forming a beautiful harmony

Waves of the Ocean

Kiss me
And explore my body
Cum in -
to me
But before you do :
Hold my hands in a way that says
" I love you
I promise not to hurt you "
Hold me like
I'm the last person you'll
ever be with
Show me your emotions
how you see this
Life with me forever ;
Please me
in a way that I won't forget
Have me coming
back to back ,
Back
for more

Kiss my neck
Mark me .
Show me .
I'm yours ,
And I'll never think otherwise

Never find a reason to hide
from you
Never find a reason to lie
to you
Always a reason to lie
with you
Hands in a Promiscuous place -
Touch you in ways that excite you .
exciting movements
Make your heart race and breath quicken
Two bodies,
One movement .
One reason .
And the words I love you .

Kiss me like you'll never see me again
Like in the morning
you don't want me to forget the feeling
of my face
against your skin

Kiss me
In missionary
Where it's your mission
to find out what's hidden
beneath my glory
Walls

damn that touch
The damn
breaks at your touch
Releasing the waves of the ocean
Awakening all my feelings
Asking you to
Cum in -
to me
and share
your deepest secrets

Cold

Each night when I can't sleep
I wish you were here for comfort
I wish you were here
so I could roll over
and feel
your body next to mine
The warmth that I desire
when I can't sleep
I desire your hand in mine
and the comfort it brings
Even if to you
those are the smallest things
To me they mean everything

Chapter Seven: Luminous

Inside

I see what you hide
behind that smile

A world full of teardrops
and raindrops.

A world full of broken hearts
and hurt.

Happiness is something you
haven't seen in a while.
You pretend to be happy,
but deep down,
you know it's all for show.

Always something on your
mind
Whether it be past, present or future.

Questions with no answers
run through your mind all day.

This leads you to confusion
And nowhere to turn.

Bare

Maybe he wants to see me naked
Hands at my sides
Everything out so that way he knows
I am comfortable

Maybe he wants to see me naked
Not my body but my soul
so that way he knows what I want
What I need
And the things that have impacted me as a human being

Maybe he wants to see me naked
Not my soul but my mind
Share everything I'm thinking
So that way he knows I have nothing to hide

Maybe he wants to see me naked
Every aspect of me
so that way he can have a better understanding
of who I am
What I'm thinking
And
what I want and need

Maybe he wants to know me

Painting

When I look at you
it's like no other

You are a painting
That I can't understand

But when I look at you
it gives me a special kind of
feeling
a feeling that I don't understand
A feeling that takes me
into a new world
A feeling that makes me
want to know more

When I look and listen to you
speak and laugh with others
I think
where did I find this one ?
where did you come from ?

There are times
when I just sit there
and think about
you
That

most definitely
puts a smile on my face
although you're colorful
and hard to embrace

But you are this incredible
painting
this work of art
So difficult to understand
So complex
and complicated
Yet when I take the time
to figure all of this out
it somehow makes
sense
this complicated work of art
with so many colors,
shapes,
figures,
splatters and stamps
this wonderful painting

As all the pieces
come together
this painting
makes sense

I almost told you "I love You." Again. for the second time . I didn't

Your heart covered in shattered
Glass
from all the people that hurt you in the
past ;

I wanna pick up every shard
and place them elsewhere .

Place them to form a beautiful
Glass
window
A place where I can view all of your beauty
but face all of your past wrongs
And the fact that no matter what
you will fuck up ,
Not intentionally
but who's to say that
life's plan isn't different than ours ?

Take those
Glass
Shards
And form a
Glass
bottle.

Where I can send all my hopes and dreams
out to sea;
Hope that one day you'll find them
but you'll already be everything I need.

Take those
Glass
Shards
and place them in the shape of a
Glass
mirror.
So you can see all the beauty
that I see
in the art that is
You.

Chapter Eight: Don't Cry

Lost

In a place unknown , everything…
Gone
No people
No houses
No buildings
No cars
No nothing
I'm lost in a place unknown
I've lost my life
Everyone I know is gone
My life is lost
I'm lost
In a place unknown
with no way out

Home ; where your heart lives

Home doesn't have to be
four walls and
a roof over your head
They say "home could be
two eyes and a heartbeat"

Your two eyes and
Your heartbeat
Was my home .
whenever I was with You ,
I Felt at home .
Home is a FEELING
I always Felt loved
I felt like I belonged
I Felt like ,
there was nowhere I'd rather be ,
than there ,
with You .

Your eyes Were my home
Whenever your eyes met mine ,
I knew that
everything was going to be alright
even if
I wasn't alright
in that moment

Your heartbeat
Was my home,
when I laid on your chest,
I heard your heart beating,
I heard the love,
as it thumped

Home doesn't have to be
four walls
Home could be someone you love
Home.
You Were my home.
You Were someone I loved.

Your hands holding mine,
Was my home.
Your voice
talking me to sleep
late at night
Was my home
Your giggles
at my annoying
and corny jokes
Was my home.
Seeing you walk around
in your socks
Was my home.

that was my comfort.
And shouldn't a home be comforting?

Knowing that whenever I called,
no matter where you were,
you Were going to answer
or I was going to get a call back
telling me you were okay
and checking on me,
telling me,
you miss me
and can't wait to see me again,
Was my home.
Your phone calls
Were my home.

You Were my home.

And just when you think your
home
is sturdy
is the same time it can collapse
unexpectedly,
Without an earthquake
or hurricane
or tsunami
The entire thing can come crashing down -

Mine Did.

My home .
Came crashing down .
right before my eyes ,
I slowly stopped getting phone calls .
You slowly stopped replying
to MY text messages
and I watched each Brick fall out of it's foundation
One by One

Now where is my Home?

Heartbroken

I've lost track of my days .
I don't even know
what month we're in .
And I don't know
whether to say
I'm going through a break up
or a heartbreak,
when I haven't fully gotten over my actual
breakup.
 And now I'm forced to go through this
heartbreak
Slash
Break Up
without being fully healed in the first place .

Although what gets me about
this one,
is that He knew
my heart
wasn't in the right place .
He knew everything
that I
put myself through
for others
He knew that I stayed up late at night
balling my eyes out

because all I could think
about was how much of a terrible person
I was
and how I wished I would've done things
differently.
I used to call him at those times.
He never hesitated to answer the phone.

He heard me cry over the phone,
over and over
because
all I heard from other people
was that,
I wasn't good enough.

He consoled my heart
at 1 o'clock in the morning
enough for me to stop crying
and enough for Him
to put me to sleep.

He knew how sensitive I was
and how when I fell for someone
I fell hard.

He knew I was falling for him
Slowly
with faith that he would catch me

But what he Didn't know
was that my heart thumped
10 times faster
when I heard his voice
and my cheeks turned ruby red
whenever He called me
while he was half asleep
because I knew
He was thinking about Me
even in the middle of the night .

What he Doesn't know is
I cry at 1 o'clock in the morning
and listen to music
to drown out the sound of my sobs .
Because I have no one else to console me ,
except for the artist's
voice coming through my blasting headphones
telling me I'm not alone .

The Stages of letting go

You'll clutch on to what you thought you had
Hold on to it by a thread

And then

Everything will slowly begin
to seem
like it's whatever.
You'll lose sight of the things
that used to make you smile,
or the people,
who used to make you smile.
You'll forget what it's like to be happy,
Maybe cry a little
And
Wonder Why
you were never good enough,

But that's all part of finding yourself.

You'll get used to nobody calling or
Texting your phone
to check on you,

Become tired of getting up
in the morning

and getting dressed,
wear sweats and not do your hair
for a while,
you'll see no point in it anymore,
There's nobody to impress

You'll want to Stay in bed
And Cry,

But eventually
You'll get tired of Sobbing
and crying.
Your emotions will be gone.
You'll only know how to smile,
to cover up any thoughts
of heartbreak
that still linger
in the back of your mind.

Smile until your mouth
Stays in that position,
Until that's all you know.
But you still won't feel a thing,

Smile until The world stops asking you,
"What's Wrong?"

Smile until Your World

Seems okay,
Smile until you look at yourself
in the mirror
and That smile
FEELS Sincere

You'll Stop Smiling
but you'll always FEEL like that smile is
there,

You'll remember what it's like to be
happy.

Stop pretending.

You realized that your pretending
Helped you
make it through,

And now you can let go of that
Person who hurt you.
You don't need them anymore
to make you smile,
You can do that yourself

Let go

Not You

I miss you.

I don't miss you.
I miss the feeling of you.
The feeling that
Someone cares for me,
as much as I care for them.
I miss the feeling
of knowing that you love me
and that all of my weirdness
would be accepted.

I miss knowing that
your feelings matched mine.
I miss the feeling of
a racing heart
And blushing cheeks,
whenever I heard your voice.

I miss the feeling of
not feeling
weird when you tell me
how much you care for me
because my feelings matched yours.

I miss the feeling

of being in your arms
and knowing that,
you would always warm me
when I was cold
or hold me when I was tired,
let me nap on your shoulder
or nuzzle into your chest.

I miss knowing that
you cared for my safety
and just wanted what was best for me.
I miss the support you gave me
whenever I needed it,

I miss the feeling of being supported
Loved
and Cared for.

But not you.
I miss the feeling of you,
Not You.

I stand before you ...

Here I stand with two roads in front
of me…
Both look like the right path.
One to the left where I stand, where
I'm at.
One to the right and I don't know
where to go.
One leads me, to me and what I
want.
I had to pick one AND Sorry
I could not travel both.
As I stand here before you I say…
I know…
And Sorry I cannot travel
both.

www.ingramcontent.com/pod-product-compliance
Lightning Source LLC
Chambersburg PA
CBHW041620220426

43661CB00049B/1550